Praise for *Time, Space, and Soul.*

*Time, Space, and Soul* is a many textured outpouring of prayer poems that contemplative mystic Ken Rosenstein has woven, the product of his own profound life-journey as a scholar of a renewed Judaism. Replete with midrashic, kabbalistic, and liturgical allusions, Rosenstein's poems are a gift of the spirit.

   — Rabbi Tirzah Firestone, author of *The Receiving*

*Time, Space, and Soul* are sacred entry points. Readers journey through each, carrying bones of ancestors past inquisition and exile toward freedom. Here the great arc of light reveals a single vibrating truth "You are there" "You are here".

   — Carol Rose, author of *From the Dream*

# Time, Space, and Soul

## A Three-Fold Cord/Chord

*(Poems for a Renewed Jewish Liturgy)*

## Ken Rosenstein

Albion
*Andalus*
Boulder, Colorado
*2014*

*"The old shall be renewed,
and the new shall be made holy."*
— Rabbi Avraham Yitzhak Kook

Albion-Andalus Inc.
P. O. Box 19852
Boulder, CO 80308
www.albionandalus.com


Design and composition by Albion-Andalus Inc.

Cover design by Sari Wisenthal-Shore.

Cover image of the oil painting, "Sensorium Dei" by Josh Goldberg (www.joshgoldbergtucson.com) used with permission.

Drawing of "Ken Rosenstein" by Netanel Miles-Yépez.


Manufactured in the United States of America

**ISBN-13: 978-0692222669 (Albion-Andalus Books)**
**ISBN-10: 0692222669**

This first volume of poetry is dedicated
with love and profound appreciation to:

Reb Zalman Schachter-Shalomi
Reb Daniel Siegel
Reb Hanna Tiferet Siegel
Reb Marcia Prager
Rachel Eryn Kalish
Charna Rosenholtz
Reb Tirzah Firestone

And in loving memory of:

Morissa Lou Williams z"l
Dear friend, poet, publisher, journalist,
champion of justice and *tikkun 'olam*

Morris Fry z"l
Dear friend who looked forward to
the publication of this volume

Just as this volume was being published,
my beloved *rebbe*, Reb Zalman Schachter-Shalomi z"l,
to whom this book is lovingly dedicated left this world.
May the memory of this holy *tzaddik* continue to be a blessing.
These poems reflect the indelible influence that he graced upon
me. I gratefully add his name to those of my dear friends
Morris Fry and Morissa Lou Williams.

# CONTENTS

## SPACE

## SOUL

# ACKNOWLEDGMENTS

For their encouragement and support of the creative process, I gratefully acknowledge: Reb Daniel Siegel and Reb Hanna Tiferet Siegel of B'nai Or of Boston who first published many of my poems, Julie Leavitt, Meri Blye Kramer, Reuven Goldfarb, Rachel Eryn Kalish, Rodger Kamenetz, Reb Laura Duhan Kaplan, Reb Tirzah Firestone, Reb Elliot K. Ginsburg, Reb Karen Landy, Reb Diane Elliot, Reb Itzchak Marmorstein, Reb James Stone Goodman, Reb TZiPi Radonsky, Richard Backer, Diana Lloyd, Janice Rubin, Joe Laur, Carol Rose, my brother Howard Rosenstein, and my publisher Netanel Miles-Yépez.

The following poems were first published in the following publications:

"Giving Birth: *Hanukkah*" and "Who's Out What's In" in *McCann's Poetry Society: A Journal of Poetry and Political Writing* (Morissa Lou Williams *z"l*, editor)

"For Those Who Were Lost on September 11" and "In Memoriam: *Primo Levi*" in *The Wild Swanns: A Journal of Poetry and Letters* (Morissa Lou Williams *z"l*, editor and publisher)

"The Exile and the Kingdom" in *The Jewish Calendar* 5754 1993-1994.

"Booths of the Soul: *Sukkot*" in *The Jewish Calendar* 5755

1994-1995.

"The Birth-Day of the World: *Rosh Ha-Shanah*", "Garments: *Va-Yeshev*", "A Tower of Bricks: A Tower of Strength: *Noah*", "The Staff of Aaron: *Va-'Era'*", "Light and Darkness: *Bo'*", "The Palace: *Mishpatim*", "Holy Fire: *Va-Yakhel*", and "Mother and Daughter: *Ba-Midbar*" in *Kolot Or: Voices of Light: B'nai Or of Boston Members' Newsletter.*

# Preface

Time, Space, and Soul are three fundamental dimensions of our Cosmos, spoken of in the earliest book of Jewish mysticism, *Sefer Yetzirah.*

*The Book of Ecclesiastes* or *Kohelet* (the Assembler) teaches that a three-fold cord is not easily broken. (4:12) Time, Space, and Soul constitute such a three-fold holographic cord that like a musical chord comprises separate notes that harmonize and integrate each with the other, a chord whose tones resonate throughout the universe.

For thematic purposes, my poems are arranged under this tripartite rubric, yet should be read as reflecting simultaneously this comprehensive vision.

A glossary and notes are provided at the end of the volume. It is my pleasure to share these poems with you. May they enrich your life in the dimensions of Time, Space, and Soul.

— Ken Rosenstein,
Boston, Massachusetts, 2014

# TIME

# THE BIRTH-DAY OF THE WORLD
## ROSH HA-SHANAH

### Malkhuyot

God reigned over the vast void
of empty space utter emptiness
co-existed in tandem with God's
dominion which extended over the
entire universe.

Silence: sovereign in its sceptered
solemnity suffused the cosmos
eons passed until the appointed moment
when the Torah gleamed in a corner
of the cosmos.

God saw the ram, or rather its *neshamah*
for it had yet to be embodied at the
appointed moment.
From its head
God gently detached its *shofar*.
God blew into the *shofar*
as God would later blow
the breath of life into Adam.
A *teki'ah* blast shattered the silence.
An infinitesimal point *Reishit*
Beginning emerges from the
curved confines of
the metaphysical mouthpiece.
For with *Reishit* God created the
heavens and the earth on this very day.
*Hayom Harat 'Olam.*

Today is the birthday of the world
Cosmic reverberations undulate
subatomic particles which eventually
birth the world and us into existence.

### Zikhronot

On this day God remembers
God remembers not only Sarah whose son
was spared by virtue of a now reified ram
God remembers us in this moment
as we turn as we return to Our Creator
anticipating the day when God sounds
the remaining *shofar* of that ram.

### Shofarot

*Shofarot* that once reverberated
at Sinai Torah's light piercing
our hearts that yearn for Your embrace
The sound of these *shofarot* will be
raised up uplifted as holy sparks
on that day *ba-yom ha-hu*
when God and God's Name
shall be One in all the earth

## INTERIOR MONOLOGUE
### *ROSH HA-SHANAH*

Blinding sunlight —
more brilliant than the day
when King Solomon dedicated
Your Holy Temple Where am I?
Moments ago the Leviathan
laughed merrily at my side —
both of us luxuriating since Creation
in Eden's Garden by the Tree of Life
Suddenly I find myself banished to this
desolate mountain like Hagar
abandoned in the wilderness
Yet, another kind of holiness envelops my
wooly body — shines from my horns
I feel Your Presence
*Hineni* — I am here —
waiting since Creation
and only You know why

Under my feet rock hard earth yields
(as I must yield?)
Thank God my feet don't slip
I trust in You to guide me
as one who does *teshuvah*

Voices, voices puncture my horns
like Joshua's trumpets at Jericho
A young child cries out to a man
towering above him
bound — the victim's eyes beseech
the one who grasps the blade — his father?
No! It cannot be!
Yet, my eyes do not deceive me
It is Isaac and Abraham his father
on Mt. Moriah

I must hide otherwise I will frighten them
causing Abraham's hand to fall fatally
I will conceal myself in this thicket,
undetected

Wait! Will I allow Isaac to die?
It must not be!

A gentle rustling of the leaves
will surely turn Abraham's head in my direction
I will substitute for Isaac
I will be the *korban*
the One Who Draws Near
for now I see my life's purpose
Take not your son — take me,
offer me on the altar of
Mt. Moriah where I see
the altar where priests will offer
many like me to You

Now I am seen as an angel of God
guides your hand
My body dispose of
Only one request I make of you, Abraham
Preserve my *shofarot*
One of them
as a sign of the Holy One's readiness to
turn as you turn towards the Name
in Remembrance of today's Test
My remaining *shofar*
herald the arrival of *Mashiah*

# THE LIGHT OF THE MOON
## *SELIHOT*

We have all journeyed
these twelve months
Waxing and waning as the moon *l'vanah*
She Who is also known as *Shekhinah*
Both we and She on the path of *teshuvah*
The path of answers the path of return
We to *Yah (YHVH)* and *Shekhinah*
She to *Tiferet* and *Ha-Kadosh Barukh Hu*
Sometimes we stray from the path and
We find ourselves in exile *galut*
Exiled from our Self
Exiled from our community
As the scapegoat will soon be on Yom Kippur
Exiled from the One as is *Shekhinah*

From exile *galut* we see *l'galot*
To discover, uncover, recover
Our bond to *Ha-Kadosh Barukh Hu* and *Shekhinah*
For She is the Gate
*He ha-Sha'ar Tzaddikim yavo'u vo*
Tzaddikim will enter through Her
In returning
Returning to the Womb of
She Who Births us into Self,
Into Soul, into Stillness
She leads me besides the still
Waters for Her Name's sake

# TESHUVAH, TIME, AND SPACE
## YOM KIPPUR

### Kol Nidre

In the court on high and in the court below ...
Noah covenanted with God upon the earth
Emerging from the aquatic womb over whose
Waters a dove flew olive twig in her mouth
Never to return again
But we creatures of flesh
And blood return to You
Annulling our vows before the Heavenly Court
Where Your Bow of Light shines before us
Curved light refracts in Einstein's curved space
Illumines our path to You
For everything is relative here
($E = teshuvah$ x $grace^2$)
Our missings of the mark in our eyes
A chance to begin again in Your's

### Shaharit

As Moses did ascending and descending
Yet again the Mountain seeing You
Face to Face Rays of Light of Understanding
Shone from the countenance that beheld You
Our God of 13 facets shining like the fire of
Diamonds that we mine in our hearts when we
Appear before You, before others
Made in Your image who cry out,
Isaiah's hungry, naked, oppressed

## Musaf

Curved light refracts yet again in
Einstein's curved time
Transmutes into curved iron
Bows of Hatred aiming
Ten arrows that hit their mark
Raining upon Ten Teachers of Torah
Ten aspects of God martyred
Crown to Kingship, Kings of Commentary
Dethroned the blood of Noah's covenant
Curdled: the blood of Roman hegemony
The blood of sacrificial rite:
Crimson wool tethers a white goat to life
Over the precipice she steps
Destined for 'Azaz'el
Though your misdeeds be as scarlet
They shall be white as snow
The Divine Name invoked thrice:
Past Present Future
This Day of At-One-ment

## Minhah

Golden nuggets of time are laden into the hold
Of a ship bound for Tarshish
In its belly a dove in raven's clothing sleeps
Thinking he can buy time by fleeing
Like Noah's winged messenger from
The word of the Lord
Jonah dreams he is Sinbad the Sailor
His treasure laden ship bound for home

Awakened by the Captain the prophet
Gazes into the stormy seas and discerns
His soul mirrored in its depths

Plunging down like
A deep sea diver mining pearls
Jonah is ingested by a great white fish
Created before Creation
For just this very moment

The fish swallows
Guilt, iniquity, failure and despair
Our mercurial persona emerges
A new human being
Having compassion even for
The withered gourd
The old self shriveled up so that
The new fruit may ripen
In the *sukkah*, the booth of his soul

## Ne'ilah

At the edge of the city of Nineveh
Whose inhabitants heeded the word of Jonah
A gate appears in the twilight
Sky above stars faintly outlining its form
Descendants of the one who unified
Time and space
Unlock its ink blue mysteries that tantalize
Us like twinkling stars in the vast cosmos
The realm of the One who welcomes us
Through the Gate of Heaven

# BOOTHS OF THE SOUL
## SUKKOT

Wandering
Seemingly aimlessly
In the desert of our soul
We are commanded by You
To build booths
Against the element-ary
Forces of Nature
Fears that erode our fortresses of strength
As sand that wears away mountains
Grain by grain
Doubts that invade the
Quiet space of the soul as a
Jackal that rips open a
Bedouin tent flap in the still
Of the night
Self hatred that beats down as the
Sun inflames the desert air.
And so we build
Constructing supports that
Shore us up under the
Invisible weight of the unknown
Adding leaves as Adam and Eve to
Shield our nakedness
Offering fruits of our soul
Acknowledging our growth this past year
As a tree adds another ring
Bears delicacies once again
After winter's barrenness.

Branches cut from the Tree
To be planted on *Mashiah*'s arrival
Lattice a canopy.
Our eyes glimpse hints of the black
Night filled with stars numerous
As Abraham's descendants.
We look up and know
That You are there
That You are here
In the *Sukkah* of
Our heart that only
Wishes to beat
In accord with Yours.

# THE ETERNAL RETURN
## SIMHAT TORAH

"Ben Bag Bag says: 'Turn it (the Torah) this way, turn it that way for everything is in it.'" — *Pirke Avot* 5:23

"Ten things were created on the first Shabbat eve at twilight. They are ... Some say ... the burial place of Moses." — *Pirke Avot* 5:6

Today we turn You around re-cycle You
As we do everytime we gaze into Your eyes.
Eye's like a prism refracting the light's spectrum
(Even the infrared and ultraviolet frequencies
Those that future generations shall see)
For as You God wrap Yourself in a robe of light
So we enfold ourselves in Your Parchment-Light.
We read in the Book of Words — *Devarim:*
"And no one knows his burial place to this day."
Perhaps Moses' soul returned to the Beginning
*Bereshit*   In the Beginning ...
"And God said: 'Let there be Light.'"
Sparks of Moses-Light filled Creation
Fell to Earth became imprisoned in *kelipot*
Myriads of *Mitzrayim*
That become liberated everyday
We perform a *mitzvah*

The Torah — a circle-cycle
Not the *pi* of the Greeks but the
Pi-ety of the Jews
The Circle that is the Whole
The perfect geometric form
That circle-cycles
Throughout our beings
Throughout our lives

# GIVING BIRTH
## HANUKKAH

All before me is darkness
Dark as my husband Isaac's sightless eyes
My womb inscrutable
Yet I sense two nations/natures nurturing
In that place of mercy *rehem*
Jacob and Esau struggle in the space that
Births them into Spirit and Sensuality
Israel and Greece interlocked as the two
Twisted tapers of the *havdalah* candle
And then: the separation from the watery Garden
Jacob clutching at his brother's heel
In his desperate struggle to be first
You shall be first Jacob, though at great cost
Cost to your morals: Listen:
Jacob — heel that he was pronounced:
"Potage for primogeniture"
On the heels of his brother's plea for a
Portion of porridge blood-red Esau consumed
Cost to our freedom: Listen:
Esau's descendants caged
Our bodies and souls in Egypt
*Mitzrayim* the Double Narrows so constricted
That no births were borne through the canal —
The Nile as a plague of darkness
Spread throughout the whole land

Yet: Israel had light
Creation light covenant light *brit* light
Eight days duration from that time of separation
As the knife severs flesh from the organ of generation
Revelation light as Moshe knelt before the
Bush of Burning Being Ineffable Being
Charging the one of uncircumcised lips to lead
His people from that place of darkness to new light
Cost to our faith as the light is obscured by lengthening
Shadows cast by the Cross which swallows
Us up into the deep flood of persecution
Desecration rape Talmud burning the fire
Of Inquisition scorching not
Just our bodies but our souls
Yet: within our hearts an eternal flame
A *Ner Tamid* burns radiating light
Redemption light that coalesces
Aggregates and separates into
Eight beacons that shine before me
Converging once again into a
Vision where out of the
Birth canal that is the Sambatyon River
I am born into the world forgetting all the Torah
That I learned under the Tree of Knowledge
The carob tree of Rabbi Shimon bar Yohai
Which sustained him for twelve years
Until the day when he emerged
Out of the cave-womb burning not the fields with his
Gaze but penetrating into your soul illuminating its
Deepest darkest recesses with radiant light
Shining as the *Zohar* fire in his eyes
Kindling Hanukkah tapers
Dedicated sentries who pass on
The torch to a new generation

Fire in Reb Nachman's eyes
Crystallized from torrents of despair
Yet: he crossed that bridge of faith above the flaming
River raging below tongues of chaos and fury
Molten rock hardening to inflexibility
Gazing straight ahead his eyes fixated on the
Opposite shore he journeys across the bridge
A birth canal air-anchored into
The Apple Orchard
Knowing that if he fell below
He would emerge as the
Phoenix from his own ashes as
Israel out of Europe's Oven
Flying heavenward a wiser Icarus

Swooping down into the Orchard below
Partaking of its most succulent sweetest fruit
Like Adam and Eve feasting in the Garden of Paradise

## THE TREE OF HESED AND TIF'ERET
### TU BI'SH'VAT

Beauty and compassion fall from the heavens like rain
Fructifying the Tree of *Hesed* and *Tif'eret*
Which grows in the Garden.
The Tree bears fruit filled with sweetness as a
Pomegranate filled with seeds.
Forever blooming is the Tree planted by Adam and Eve
Their final act before leaving the Garden
For they were the first caretakers
Of Mother Earth and of humanity.

Throughout the generations the Tree of
*Hesed* and *Tif'eret* of Compassion and Beauty
Gave of herself, offered her wood, her being
To Cain — the first farmer
Proffering fruit of the soil as sacrifice
To Noah — sole *paterfamilias*
Of an ecologically ravaged planet
Using her knotty skin for the water-borne Ark
To Abraham — himself a mighty oak rooted in *Hesed*
Chopping her branches for Isaac's pyre

Many such trees were planted
Wherever the Jews settled
Its fruit bore seeds that each generation
Lovingly cultivated in their adopted land
The first exiles planted the Tree in Babylon
Fertilizing the arid soil with their tears
From this holy earth the
Hanging Gardens Of Babylon sprouted
These are the towns of Sura and Pumbedita
Cradle of the Talmud
And the last generation will plant
The Tree of *Hesed* and *Tif'eret*
Before the arrival of the *Mashiah*

There exists a Tree inside each of us
We tap into the Tree as a farmer taps a
Vermont Maple in winter extracting rich nectar.
When we are fully alive in
The World of the Body
The World of the Heart
The World of the Mind
The World of the Spirit
Then the Tree of *Hesed* and *Tif'eret* grows within us.

Each Torah stave is fashioned from this Tree
For the Torah is a Tree of Life, a Tree of *Tif'eret*
The Voice of the Turtledove is heard from its branches
Singing sweet words of Torah
And when we listen, really listen
As we did at Mt. Sinai
Then we and the Tree are as one.

# Light and Gladness,
# Happiness and Honor
## *Purim*

Sunshined Shushan shimmers in
Light golden as the goblets from which
King Ahasuerus drinks

Rose-colored Jerusalem stone radiates
Rubylight refracts from harem windows
Illuminating maiden's faces
Rouge-flushed courtesy of
Revlon and Estée Lauder

Feasting his eyes on the delicacies arrayed
Before him the Potentate of Persia ponders:
Who will be Queen for the day
(And perhaps longer?)
The greater light to rule by day
Brilliant as the sun
Hides her true identity behind a veil
Fuchsia-hued as the Torah secrets her
Riches deep inside
Fine gold more precious than rubies
The lesser light to rule by night
As his sleep was disturbed
For did not the King recollect
That to Mordecai the Jew he was in debt?

Blackest night shrouds the city of Shushan
As we are at our mortal end
Blacker still the heart of one
Pernicious plans woven as a
Black widow spider spins her web
From which there is no escape

A new day dawns on the dozing denizens
Golden rays cleave the darkness like
King Arthur's sword
Wrested from Excalibur
On the streets below a crowd gasps:
For who appears on a royal steed but
Mordecai bedecked in robes of royalty
Led by none other than the Vile Vizier
Venom on his tongue as he proclaims:
"This is what is done for the man whom
The King delights to honor."

But the King must succor
The Scheming Scoundrel
Such is his wife's modest desire
Her words music to his ears
As the dulcet tones of King David's lyre

The Fanatical Fiend is fed
Not once but twice glory going to his head
Suddenly, Esther unmasks Hated Haman
Revealing her lineage
For it was her people the Jews
That the Agagite wished to pillage

His thoughts naked as the day he was born
Heathen Haman is held up to scorn
Upon the gallows prepared for the Jew
The Despotic Despoiler is hung for
All to view

The enemies of the Jews prepare to battle
As swords clash and sabers rattle
The tables are turned as dice in the hand
The descendants of Benjamin rejoice
Throughout the land

Our tale concluded for all to applaud
Praise and thanks to You, O God

# RITE OF PASSAGE
## PESAH

And a new king rose over Egypt
Who knew not the children of
Joseph the Provider
Growing and multiplying in the
Land of the Double Narrows
They became as numerous as the stars of
The night sky thats once bowed down to
The comely youth
The Potentate proclaiming:
"The strangers shall be under my rod
Their eldest male newborn
Spirited away by the Nile."
So that amongst its reeds
Moses was concealed like the 'afikoman
Cradled in a basket borne by the Nile:
"One day, for your sake, I will crimson my
Waters the color of your swaddling blanket
So that your people, your blood,
May run
Free."

From out of the fire that forged a people
Like a Japanese samurai sword ready to
Cleave obstacles like the waters of the
Reed Sea the Voice that spoke to Moses:
"I AM THAT I AM"
For only in liberation in fire does a people
Emerge as you have, Moses on this Mountain
Emerge from the flames of My House on
Zion not once, but twice
Emerge from tongues of flame that licked
Masada's fortress
Emerge from charred ruins of medieval
Ghettoes and souks
Emerge between the Talmud folios
Black fire on black pages
Letters aloft curlicues of *'alef-bais*
That linger still in the Venetian sky
Above the palace of Doge
Emerge from the blood soaked soil of Europe
The soul of a continent extinguished
As the match that lights
*Shabbat* candles in the barracks at Auschwitz
Emerge as Abraham from the fiery furnace

Whose grandson Jacob, tricked by a
Wandering Aramean went down to that
Strange land where his son reigned like the
Sun in the midday sky that
Darkened when Pharaoh built his cities
And monuments by the sweat of our brow
So that our cries reached the ears of the
King of Kings above Pharaoh whose own
Ears were stuffed with the cotton of
Self-righteousness so that only plagues
Descending on Egypt like his royal
Taskmaster's lashes on our backs
Drawing blood that infiltrated the Nile
Could move he that reigned from Memphis to Thebes
To let our people go

And only after the
Avenging Angel of Annihilation
Passed over our homes lintels reddened
From sacrificial lambs forever stifling the
Cries of the Egyptian firstborn
Did we embark on our journey towards
Freedom so hurried were we that our
Dough had no time to rise, to become
Completed, for we to become
Completed so we settled for thin crackers
That broke in our hands like the chains of slavery
This Bread of Affliction that one declared his body
Wine consumed in haste made from grapes
Of wrath that one declared his blood
Our enemies charging that we need it to
Bake our Bread of Pain that conceals our
Stories in its perforated crevices like
Integrated chips storing myriads of memory

Memories that sustained us 40 years like
The *manna* heaven sent tasting of the
Rebbe's *challah* at *shalosh seudos*
Eliyahu Ha-Navi regaling us with his tales
In his hands the Cup is raised
Visions of Rabbis teaching Torah to
Generations not yet born their insights
Originating from Moshe Rabbenu
Himself at Mt. Sinai who witnessed the
Death of Rabbi Akiva
Combs tearing at strands of memory
That refused to break
Declaring the poem of two lovers
In the Galilee our holiest book
Which speaks of a love that springs eternal
From the hearts of these two
Whom Moses glimpsed from
The summit of Mt. Nebo
Just as his soul expired
The kiss of God on his lips

## OF PYRAMIDS AND LATTICES

A rainbow arcs across the sky
Colors of Joseph's coat
Our ancestor whose bones we would carry
Offer to God like Abraham's Isaac in our
Own land if only we could whose presence
Would be sensed among us like a
Pillar of Cloud by Day,
A Pillar of Fire by Night

Dewdrops of freedom bathe our bodies
Well up within us like the Nile whose
Waters rise imperceptibly until one fateful
Day when they overflow their banks

Embers of independence kindled within
Our hearts as searing desert air scorches
Our lungs   vibrates in tune to pent up
Sighs longings to be released from
Egyptian imprisonment entombed as their
Dead Pharaohs mummified kings sleep
Eternally beneath massive pyramids
Whose apex points to an open vault
Cerulean blue that mirrors our yearning to
Be free back into our hearts
Hearts that beat in rhythm to a different
Beat the clash of tambourine skins against
The hand of a prophetess
Who leads us with her brothers
Moses and Aaron

He who was drawn from the river
Drew us forth from the Sea of Reeds
Seas that birthed us on to dry land
Silenced triumphant cries
The hopes of pursuers drowned
Buried forever as their sun worshipers
Akhnaten's acolytes

Our souls wept bitter tears of salt water
Transformed to fine frost overnight
We feasted on *manna* the next day

Days drenched in honey
Oh yes, they were
Gossamer sweet
Our souls peeked through
Torah-lettered
Honeycomb  lattices
*Shekhinah* winks at us
As honey-golden Light
Flows throughout our bodies
For we are home
For we are home

# THE 33<sup>RD</sup> DAY
## LAG B'OMER

A Promethean Angel streaks across
Ink blue mystery bearing
Black Fire on White Fire she cradles the
Divine Gift to her bosom as a mother her
New born babe before relinquishing
Her Treasure to the two secreted at the
Mouth of Meron's cave on Earth below
A subterranean womb *in potentia*
Incubator of incomparable incunabula
R. Shim'on b. Yohai and his son Eliezer
Await the angelic annunciation
As Abraham and Sarah
"Will one such as myself give birth to
Splendor such as this?"
As R. Shim'on laughs the Messenger
Delivers her embered embryo to
The two of them with a Mona Lisa
Smile and flies away
The moon shines on the cave of Meron
Twelve months times twelve
Twelve cycles of the Zodiac which
Twinkles in the black vault

"Unto us a child is born" on
The 33<sup>rd</sup> day of the Omer
As the couple emerge from their exile
The whole world is aflame from their
Teaching that burns not fields with its heat
But illumines the dark recesses of the heart
With its brilliance as a cavern lit by a
Beacon a bonfire whose holy sparks flutter
Ever higher into the cosmos waiting to be
Redeemed

On that day students of the one who
Entered and exited *PaRDeS* alive
Fought against the pagan eagle who
Darkened *Shekhinah*'s wings
Hoping for deliverance by Bar Kochba
Son of a Star that sparkles in the heavens
From whence came that Angel

On that day She appeared one final time
Bearing the soul of he who revealed
Secrets of Torah to us
We wait for Redemption still as
Stars beckon in the twilight sky
Illuminating the Universe with their
Radiance

# Standing at Mt. Sinai
## *Shavu'ot*

A Mountain looms over us
Immense, towering filling creation
Sheer rock, hard as diamond
But not yet as crystal clear
As the Revelation that will
Emanate from its fiery peak
The Mountain: on fire
Fire of passion
Divine passion, our passion
For each other
We the Bride
God the Bridegroom
Between us: the Torah
Our *ketubah*
Black fire on white fire
The Mountain: aflame
Our love a burning flame
And the bush was not consumed

Suddenly, SIlence
The Silence of 'Aleph
Not "'Adonai'", not "'Anokhi'"
Or "Ah"
Just Silence
Filling our bodies as
God filled Creation with
Divine Light at the
Beginning
In the Beginning was the 'Aleph
The Light that Adam saw
Messianic Light
One gigantic 'Aleph
That contracted
Made room for the world

We are overwhelmed
And then:
The Hearing: the I
We know that we will do
We don't even have to hear
(But it helps)

The Voice: It
Shatters us and the
Mountain into
600,000 fragments
(more than 600,000)
That we redeem every day
We invoke God's Name
Following Divine Instructions
Repairing the shattered world

The Mountain:
A Mirror
In which we see our
Truest selves
Reflected
Every time
We cleave to
Our mate.

## DIAMONDS FROM DUST
## TISH'A' B'AV

'*Eikha* — How?
The Scroll of Lamentations begins
How? On this day
Could we bear to see our city
Aflame?
How? Could the Nazis
Destroy a people
A culture
Burnt to ashes?
How? Could America drop a portable
Death factory incinerate a city?
Jerusalem '*Ir shalem*
A City
Of peace that
Consumed itself because of
Baseless hatred
Flames of Jealousy, Hate, Anger
Our spiritual center, the Temple ablaze
No, the center of the world, *axis mundi*
Off-course, out of orbit, revolving
Somewhere in our galaxy like a
Mis-programmed satellite
Our bodies — individual temples
Worn out, exhausted polluted with
Cigarettes, orange-flamed at the tip
Incinerated to carbon-ash in a minute
Like the residents of
Hiroshima and Nagasaki

We create our own exile
From ourselves, our truest nature
Longing for the center, we see a vision:
The Temple burns
We feel the heat — hotter than the
H Bomb interior hotter than Auschwitz
Transmute the base carbon elements of
Anger, Jealousy, Hate to
Diamonds of Calm, Charity, Love
The flames reach higher into the Cosmos
Becoming Holy Sparks in the rarefied air
Flying Heavenward as the letters of
R. Hananiah b. Teradyon
Liberated from the confines of the Torah
Scroll in which he was wrapped, a martyr
For we know:
The flaming swords that block
Our way to the Garden
Are the same ones we use to
Carve out passageways into the
Garden of the Text the *PaRDeS*
That brings us back home from exile
From the exile of the text, of the kingdom
For today is not any day, no
Today is the birthday of the *Mashiah*
Hope's embodiment our deliverer from
The bondage of hate, jealousy, apathy
An eschatological Moses who kindles
The passion for love, justice, compassion
The One Who lives in us

# THE ASCENT:
## BERESHIT

Once upon a time (when time began, that is) there lived a man named Earth-Being for he was made of the earth. The garden was Paradise to the man and he was very happy. So happy that he wanted to share his happiness with another just like him but not <u>exactly</u> like him. (You know what I mean, don't you?) So the One Who created the Earth-Being created also a mate named Living-Being for only she could bring life to the man, complement his life, complete his life.

The man and the woman were very happy playing together in the garden like children. Until one day, when the man and the woman were walking together in the garden, they passed by the Tree of Knowledge of Good and Bad. Something stirred in both of them at that moment. A great desire each for the other filled their beings. They gazed into one another's eyes but did not know what to do for they had not yet eaten of the fruit of the Tree. An intense hunger rose in them. They picked the fruit from the Tree and ate. (No, there was no snake in the garden in this story. This is Paradise, remember?) Eating, the eyes of the two of them were opened and they knew what they must do. The man formed a sheath from a thin leaf and wrapped it around the part of his body that made him a man for he was not yet ready for his seed to enter the woman, only his love. And so, the man entered the woman, all of the man's being, his essence channelled into her. The woman, she too bonded with the man and they became as one. The lives of both of them were now complete. They knew also that they could share the garden with others to come after them though the price be their eventual death. For new life comes only from death and Paradise would not be Paradise were only the two of them to share it forever.

The Creator saw that the man and the woman had outgrown the garden. The Creator led the two of them out of the garden, lovingly. The gates to the garden were closed, not locked. For all may enter the garden whenever they wish. The man and the woman bid farewell to the garden and opened their eyes to the world.

Now some call this story The Fall from Grace, *Hesed*. But know that the deepest act of *Hesed* was the man and the woman loving as one. For out of this union emerged others, just like them to fill the earth, to tend the garden.

# GARMENTS:
## VA-YESHEV

It could be argued that Israel wove
Joseph's destiny just as he had
Joseph's coat of many colors:
radiant hues of the *sefirot*
(for each *sefirah* has a color)
reflected God's glory blinded the brothers
to the true nature of their sibling the *tzaddik*
for without that stained cloak stained
with jealousy as much as with blood
the brothers would have no ruse
on which to hang their deception:
deception that prefigured Joseph's fate yet once
again as Potiphar's wife seduced
by that Hebrew's sexuality
(the foundation of all/life)
held his fate in her hands his tunic
Ironic is it not that Joseph had to be stripped
of his outer garments so as to
reveal his true nature:
the garments of his soul at
just the right moment?

# A TOWER OF BRICKS:
# A TOWER OF STRENGTH
## NOAH

Babylon's black-hearted potentate a
prototypical Pharaoh rebelled against God
Nimrod — he whose ego blazed
as the midday sun erected
a tower to his name
a tower of bricks baked by
the scorching rays of the sun
bricks seared by the fires of
competition of hatred of hubris
For Nimrod would not be challenged
Only one would utter God's truth
black fire on white fire blazed from the
eyes of Abram as he confronted the one
who idolized fire — fire which hardened
Babel's bricks fire which hardened
Nimrod's heart so that Abram was
consigned to fire — not even the fire of
devotion in Abrams' heart would save him
so God dispatched Gavriel the mighty
*malakh* messenger of God to deliver him

Abram looked at Nimrod's tower
as his subjects scattered in confusion for their
competition cruelty calumny consigned them
to the far corners of the world
Abram mused: My descendants shall
build not towers of brick
rather they shall construct towers
of spice boxes for *havdalah*, towers of strength,
towers of learning, towers of mysticism
whose windows open not upon *Bab-El*
rather upon the Gate of the One

# THE STAFF OF AARON
## VA-'ERA'

It was evening and it was morning:
the sixth day
twilight the cusp of *Shabbat*
amongst the ten things that were created:
the rod of Moses, and others say:
also the staff of Aaron
both fashioned from the Tree of Life
and the Tree of Knowledge of Good and Bad
(how else would Moses our Teacher
and Aaron the High Priest have been
sustained for 40 years in the desert?)
the staff of Aaron shone as the light of
Creation's first day: for it was adorned
with the gems of his breastplate jewels
which reflected God's glory God's *Hod*
blinded Pharaoh and his magicians so that
Aaron's serpentine staff consumed those
of the Oppressor a primordial snake slithered
from the Tree of Knowledge to the River Nile
in an act of *teshuvah* for the glory of God
for the glory of Aaron the archetype
of *Hod* who ascended to the Heavenly Temple
the Celestial Court at Mt. Hor
40 years after his appearance at
the idolator's court

The Sages teach: Do not read Mt. Hor
rather Mt. Hod for upon this mountain
those who seek God's glory shall be
guided by the staff of Aaron

## LIGHT AND DARKNESS
### Bo'

From the land of Egypt God's Presence withdrew
alighted on locusts' wings flew
Heavenward secreted itself for three days
in the Palace of Light above
the Hidden Light of the Righteous
illuminated the dwellings of the
Israelites in Goshen
However darkness
insunuated itself insidiously in
the hovels of Egyptian laborers
in the mansions of Egyptian ministers
in the Palace of Pharaoh below
Darkness eclipsed the sun banishing
Helios into exile the spirit of Akhnaten
scatters as the rays of that obscured star
Darkness so thick it nearly suffocated the
Egyptians, nearly, for the Avenging Angel
of Annihilation lay in wait secreted within the darkness
those three days awaiting the word of the One who alone
commands him "Consecrate to me every first born
(man and beast) the first issue of every womb among
(the Egyptians) is Mine."
As the Israelites offered their first fruits
their *bikurim* on the Feast of Matzot
so were the first born Egyptians offered,
sacrificed as the Avenging Angel of
Annihilation slit their throats

Blood spurted on to doorposts and lintels
reddened door-frames consanguinated
scarlet adorning door-frames of the Israelites
the prototypical *mezuzah*
minus the words (those would come later)
for they shall be a sign upon our hand and
between our eyes words that would remind us
of this night of vigil, a *leil shimurim*
words that, writen on our hearts,
consecrate us to the One who
forms light and creates darkness

# THE PALACE
## *MISHPATIM*

A sunlit sky scintillates sparkles as
radiant diamonds
Primordial light of creation's first day
suffuses the heavens
Alights on the faces of Moses, Aharon,
Nadav, Abihu and the 70 elders
They who would one day represent the
70 nations
They who would one day identically
translate *lashon ha-kodesh* into the
languages of nations
The pillar of our people erected an altar:
12 pillars signifying 12 tribes: a sign of the
Zodiac on each one for God's Presence
shines in the constellations above as it
does on the Earth below: the whole world
is full of God's glory
Moshe Rabbenu, Aharon the High Priest
Nadav, Abihu and the 70 elders soared on
*Shekhinah*'s wings to the celestial Palace
that shone with the light of the *sefirot*
Our spiritual witnesses beheld rooms and
chambers revealing
secrets of the Holy One
They ate and drank nourishing their souls
with fruit plucked from the Tree of Life
water from the stream in 'Eden

In the center of the Palace, jewelled
Tablets of Torah radiated Holy Light
For they were inscribed by the *Shekhinah*
white fire on white tablets
A cloud obscured Her for 6 days
6,000 years of exile
On the 7th day She re-appeared
rested refreshed
*Shekhinah* called to Moses
She calls to us

# HOLY FIRE
## VA-YAKHEL

"You shall kindle no fire throughout
your settlements on *Shabbat.*"
Rather, the fire of devotion, of *devekut*
kindled in your hearts on this day
shall suffice; for you who cleave unto God
are alive this day
the fire for the altar of sacrifice shall not
burn on *Shabbat* for your prayer, your
*mitzvot,* your study shall be your offering
your *korban* on this day
for the world is sustained by these three
pillars that support the *mishkan*
no less than the planks of acacia wood
hewn from the Tree of Life for
She the Torah is a Tree of Life for
all who cleave to Her
Her Black Fire on White Fire shall
ignite your hearts your souls when you
write Her words on your hearts on your
souls this day

Her words your words shall ascend as
the fragrant incense on the altar a sweet
savor to God redolent of the *besamim*
in *Gan 'Eden* (for there never was to be a
*havdalah* in that earthly paradisal *mishkan):*
Adam and Eve driven out before *Shabbat*
wafted in the cool of the evening:
Adam and Eve escorted by the *Shekhinah*
all in exile: hence a *mishkan ba-midbar*
a *mishkan* situated in the desert for
*Shekhinah* must dwell now at this moment
between the *keruvim* who flew from their
posts at the Tree of Life to dwell to settle
here above the Ark as they gaze
at one another as Adam and Eve
in *Gan 'Eden*

# THREADS OF LIFE
## *KI TISA'*

The delicate scent of incense
Permeates the air
Myrrh and frankincense commingle in this
Space our sanctuary built of us from the
Smallest to the greatest
Robed in majesty and splendor
In wisdom and understsnding
Aaron the High Priest stands before us
Arrayed in a mantle of Light
Primordial Light suffuses us as at the Beginning
The brazier's flame reflected in his eye
The flame that ignited the Burning Bush
Fires the altar of our hearts which serve
The One Who Is, Was, Will Be
Oil and water flow over the head of Aaron
The proto Messiah as *halakhah* and *aggadah*
Consecrating him consecrating us when
We flow with the currents of law and
Legend that course throughout our History
Streams of consciousness that undulate
Quiescently beside our vines and fig trees
Planted by still waters
We sleep unafraid for we have plucked
Rich fruit from that Tree of Knowledge
That Tree of Life whose wood provided
Planks for our sanctuary fashioned by
Bezalel he who crafts in the shadow of God
In the shadow of God we fashion our lives
Weaving together life's delicate threads
The warp and the woof of *halakhah* and *aggadah*

The crimson of passion the blue of quiet
Intellect the silver that roots us to this
Earth the gold that radiates throughout our
Lives when our eyes are as open as
Moses' were on that Mount 40 days and
40 nights his face radiant as the
Gold Letters engraved on the Rock that is our
Being seeing ourselves face to face as
Moses beheld You in the cleft of the Rock
Your Presence filled the place as the Place
Was with the Servant of God shielded by
The Hand that fashioned us all out of the
Red clay from the four corners of the
World breathing into our nostrils the
Breath of life a covenant fashioned that
Day between You and me
On that day we put on our finery and
Embraced Your Teaching:
The Breath of Life is in those whose
Livelihood is not gained at the expense of
Others as a kid boiled in its mother's milk
The Breath of Life is in those who are
Nourished by unleavened bread whose
Hubris does not rise as the yeast in the dough

The Breath of Life is in those who sow
Seeds of creativity offering the first fruits
Of their labor their finest work
Harvesting when it is ripe
The Breath of Life is in those who
Honor the Shabbat Queen
The Breath of Life is in those whose hands
Are full of God's Work as the
Pomegranate is full of seeds

Golden Light shone from the face of
Moses the Light that God created before
Creation filled our beings that day
Annointed in the Light as Aaron and
David we greeted each other face to face
And dwelt in the Sanctuary of our Heart

# THE EIGHTH DAY
## SHEMINI

Implacable mountains belie their rose patina
as dawn's light caresses the
Israelite encampment nestled below in
the womb of the desert
As a new born infant is ushered into the
*brit* eight days after emerging from the womb
so were Aaron and his sons initiated
into a *brit* on the eighth day
Nadav and Abihu — perhaps Judaism's first
innovators by their offering of alien fire —
a fire not commanded by God but nevertheless
heart-felt as Jeremiah's *brit chadashah*
a circumcision of the heart
the passion of Nadav and Abihu so inflamed
that it consumed their reason
their judgement so that they became an
'*olah* a burnt offering a conflagration so
intense that matter and antimatter collided
imploded upon the burning of the incense
*Hitlahavut* divine enthusiasm and Dionysian excess
face to face in a fatal embrace
thus they died at the instance of *YHVH*
the anger that immolated
Sodom and 'Amorah now visited
upon the sons of Aaron — not the fire of
Revelation on Mount Sinai but the fire of
fury that would one day ravage Jerusalem's diadem
The Holy Temple a refined and adorned
daughter of the *mishkan* secreting
*Shekhinah* who weeps in a desolate corner

Her tears dried by the cloak of Elijah
the Prophet whose presence envelops a
newborn into the covenant
He who heralds the coming of *Mashiah*
cradles the souls of Nadav and Abihu
who perished for the sanctification of
THE NAME borne aloft in his chariot
awaiting the opening of
the Gates of Heaven

## MOTHER AND DAUGHTER
### BA-MIDBAR

A wrathful sun sears the desert sky
to instantaneous incandescence
bakes silica saturated sand supporting
*Shekhinah*'s standard bearers for
twelve flags: banners and standards of
every color, every design, every thought
and every emotion
testify to the loyalty of these twelve tribes
constellated around the Levites who guard
the *Mishkan* as *Yah*'s *keruvim* protected
the Tree of Life
Levi's descendants are consecrated to God
(as are we) for they are progeny of Dinah's
brother of she whose honor would be avenged
of she whose name signifies
judgement
*Shekhinah* weeps for Dinah's defilement
as Her *Shekhinah*'s heliotropic consort
blazes in Her abode
the troops are mustered — the census has
numbered as *Yah* commanded Moses

# RAV KOOK POEM CYCLE

## 1

Infinity secretes herself within the rings
the *'egoolim* circle cycles concentrically
arrayed in the *kodesh kodashim* of
these towering redwoods
"Where were you when my seeds were
implanted deep in the earth womb?
Like the *kav* plumb line of infinite light
I impregnate Gaia — the Earth, fructify it
with my seed rooted in Her soil as my
*komah* stature testifies to upright *kivun*
intention direction in-line with You."

— August 15, 2006

## 2

Your Light hidden *'or ha-ganuz*
it is said for the righteous *la-tzaddikim*
in the world to come *b'olam ha-ba'*
the world too that is hidden
in this world as the Maiden in the Tower
When will I enter Her secreted chambers
When will She *Shekhinah* disclose Her mysteries to me?
*Nafshi cholat ahavatekhaikh*
*'Or ha-ganuz nigleh be-gan ha-'egozim*
The Hidden Light is revealed in the Garden of Nuts
The Garden of Torah

may its secrets crack out of their *kelipot*
their shells that obscure the Light
may its light penetrate my soul as the
*kav 'or 'ein sof* impregnates the
Garden of *Shekhinah*

— August 16, 2006

## 3

The snake coiled itself around the orbs of
potentiality strangling articulation of the
light secreted within the Tree of
Knowledge of Vision and Blindness
Sparks of Light fell from infinities of
laddered chambers palaces of messianic
potentialities quantum visions holographic
*heikhalot* waiting to be uplifted by souls
free of serpentine deception

— August 17, 2006

4

Without hope I will die
The Tree of Life, The Tree of Knowledge
of Good (never mind the evil)
Banish the evil I am so tired of it
and how do I live with what the rabbis called
my *yetzer ha-ra'* or as Reb Jung would say
my *yetzer ha-tzel?*
I am so tired in my struggle with it
for it is not only the shadow in my psyche
but the over-shadow that occluded the light
for we see through a mirror darkly from Moshe on
Those 2 Trees root me to this Earth
*'Eretz zavat chalav u-devash*
I need to stay connected to the flow,
the *shefa'* or else I will die
apple tethered to the branch tether of life
*'Etz Hayim hee la-mahazikim bah*
She is a Tree of Life for those
who hold fast to Her

— August 18, 2006

# FOR THOSE WHO WERE LOST ON SEPTEMBER 11

As the Holy Temple burned
The High Priest consigned the keys to its door heavenward
A Divine Hand emerged from above and
clasped them to its Heart

As the Twin Towers burned
Millenia later
God *Allah* the Holy Ghost
*Shekhina Shikeina*
Unlock the keys to **our** hearts

Tears rain down
Upon the smoldering ruins
Of desecrated ground of hallowed ground
Of holocausted ground

By the waters of the Hudson
we lay down **and** wept
By the waters of the Potomac
we lay down and wept
By the waters of Stoney Creek
we lay down and wept

Weeping

For those lost on that day
Weeping even more for those 19
whose souls were so lost to God
before that day had even dawned
that they felt their only option lay in
losing their lives and thousands upon thousands
of innocent victims

May the tears that fall upon Ground Zero
May the tears that bathe the Pentagon
May the tears that shower that field in
Shanksville, Pennsylvania

Be not only tears of sorrow of pain
of anguish of depair of rage but ultimately
tears of understanding of commitment of
reconciliation the tears of Jacob and of Esau who wept
upon each other's necks
after half a lifetime of estrangement

# 1620

A presence is sensed on the horizon
as the calm waters of the Atlantic undulate uneasily the
Mayflower dwarfs canoes that
bob in the water
Strangers garbed in black emerge from the fragile vessel
beached on the old-new land
Garbled sounds fill pristine air
destined to become smog-laden centuries hence

Eyes peer out from behind trees that hide bodies colored as
clay iron-red bodies that
became as clay in the hands of those whose ancestors
stood by the shore where
the water lapped against the Rock

Freedom sprouted tender as the corn that
dared to pierce New England soil hardened
by black leather boots
Freedom that withered and died soon after
in the winter of their discontent
Our hosts forgotten banished like our
conscience to far flung outposts of the mind that only
remembers, resurrects an
image every now and then
"Be fruitful and multiply," we were told
and we multiplied
having dominion over the land and we dominated

# Ken Rosenstein

On this day of non-domination
this secular Sabbath let us give thanks
For those who welcomed us
For the land which has supported us
For the people who have
pilgrimaged here since
For the lives we lead this day

— Thanksgiving Day, 1991

# SPACE

# FOUR PLACES

## 1
### *Magritte's Castle*

A castle floats above the Pyrennes
A pipe awaits its owner this day
But it isn't really a pipe, you see
Only a representation of reality
Bouldered Brits rain from the sky
Without even knowing the reason why
A train travels through time and space
Emerging from a fireplace
An apple is conjured from up a sleeve
A hologram appears of Adam and Eve
Through whose transparent bodies
Glimpses of The Tree tantalize
Visions of the Truth materialize

## 2
### *K's Forest*

The Tree which barricades its knowledge
Behind the guarded doors of that Pyrenean
Castle impregnable fortress of the Psyche
(If Eden had sheltered The Castle
Would Kafka had written *The Tree?*)
Does bowlered Franz descend from the
Firmament above sheltering us with his love?

## 3
### Baudelaire's City

City streets snake into labyrinths where
Green-eyed vipers proffer verdant fruit for
Our eyes that gleam in the darkness of the
Night concealing fear, hiding fright
While others greet the light of day
Someone waits for Joseph K.

## 4
### Borges' Library

Who can be found this moment
Hunched over a tome of philosophy
Having exhausted himself and all possible
Legal remedies our hero finds comfort in
The thoughts of thinkers whose words
Have yet to be indicted on pristine paper
Thoughts known only to souls hovering
Above castles in the air overlooking
Trees of Knowledge from whose branches
Could be glimpsed the horizon of
The City of God

# WHO'S OUT WHAT'S IN

This morning THE BOSTON GLOBE
featured a story about the completion of the
Brookline-Brighton-Newton 'eruv
a device whereby open spaces are closed
by wire — fences, twine, cable what have you
thus creating a boundary which serves to extend an
observant Jew's private domain
thereby allowing for the use and
transport transfer of objects
on the Sabbath the day of rest
An interesting paradox:
wires that enclose a space open up possibilities,
freedom of movement for those in that very space
logic that turns in my mind as a Möbius strip

This afternoon at the Brookline Booksmith
my eye catches the title of a new book
by the Israeli author of The Yellow Wind
David Grossman Sleeping on a Wire:
Conversations with Palestinians in Israel
For Palestinian, read Arab (in Hebrew: 'aravi)
that is to say: Israeli Arabs
Citizens of Israel
They alone are not on the high wire —
so are we both of us precariously
perched high above the circus below
My eyes stare into his:
Careful Don't fall For if
you fall, I fall as well

This evening (in Hebrew: 'erev)
I read late into the night
And I remember: Before we
were Jews, we were Hebrews ('Ivrim)
those who transferred from one land to
that land some of whose descendants
would "transfer" Israeli Arabs over to Jordan
as easily as one transfers keys to a pocket
within an 'eruv

'Aravi 'Ivri 'Eruv 'Erev
Transpose Transfer

It's only a matter of changing/exchanging
one letter (life) for another
Or two Or three

— February 10-15, 1993

# The Exile and the Kingdom

On wings of eagles have you flown home
My brothers and sisters from the land of
Your mother's birth     Queen of Sheba
She who was black and comely
Left her homeland journeying
Many days to behold and match wits
With the King of Wisdom     Solomon
Shelomo who was not whole until
He joined his being exiled many years
Ago to hers welding together two peoples
Like the *Beta Yisra'el* weld iron
Fashioning crafts for tourists in
Gondar Province
The Lion of Judah purrs contentedly from
His underground lair:
"My people have arrived,
My people have come home."

— June 1, 1991
One week after the completion of
Operation Solomon

# SOUL

# THE STILL SMALL VOICE

The two that are one
Separate and equal
Joined at the generating centres of their beings
Giving and receiving
Unbroken chain reaction
Producing sparks of electricity lightning
Flashes of passion
Thunderous reverberations
And then
A still small voice
God
Not in the fire
Or the thunder
But in the cleft of the rock
In the still small voice
Whispering within two hearts
That beat as one

## HOMAGE TO VINCENT

Starry night beacons of inspiration
Pierce the darkness of your soul
Paint thrown at canvas chaotically
Metamorphoses into compositions
Of grandeur architecture in pigment
Cathedrals of quietude
Tortured landscapes of the soul
Personless vast panoramas
Piercing stillness wounding your soul
That transcends the pain by
Illuminating our lives
Sun casting elegiac shadows
Guiding our steps by a lone
Cherry blossom tree
A yellow house incubating our bodies
Cocooning us un a bed
As wide as the universe that
Never loved you for you
So that one July day in that ravaged
Wheatfield canopied by an angry violet
Sky crows screeching imprecations you
Let fall your brush impregnated with color
To the ground embracing the earth
Scarlet seeping into the ochre
Burnt sienna soil your visions relinquished
To that starry night forever

# FRUIT

Ripe rubicund fruit
Held in your hand
Held inside you
Fruit of the tree
Fruit of two
Who lay under that tree
In the cool of the day
Whose setting sun
The color of that fruit
Deep inside
Warmed you both
With a tenderness
That flows from your eyes
(Like the river that nourishes the tree)
To the one you love
Transfixing you
A moment in time
For eternity

# ON READING THAT THE NOVELIST JERZY KOSINSKI IS FOUND DEAD IN HIS BATHTUB APPARENTLY A SUICIDE MAY 4, 1991

Why did you do it, Jerzy K.?
Joseph K. had others accuse him but
Your accusations welled up from within
The mind that was so ingenious it could trick
The Party into allowing a non-existent scientist
To fly to this land of freedom it was your only way in
Accusations welled up from within the mind
That conjured up Chauncey Gardiner
By Chance we were tricked into
Believing he could be the next President
Whose world was encompassed by the
Square confines of a TV screen and
Whose metaphor for life was a garden
But your mind found no way out of a
body that was not at the peak of perfection
Like your polo player athlete:
The painted bird inside you spiraled
From the sky above and landed in a bathtub
Its voice muted like the child you once were
A plastic bag around its head
Permitted no inspiration to reach your mind
Your heart that beat somewhat
Irregularly that should not have bothered
You a man who survived Nazi occupied Poland
Polish Communism by not
Conforming being slightly out of step

Steps that parted you from your language
Your manners your belongings thirty four
Years ago now led to your final place of rest
May it be in a garden where the lilacs are ever in bloom
The flowers full and open
The grass a verdant carpet
The sky above ever so blue and bright
Filled with the colors of painted birds

— May 16, 1991

# LENNY

Black notes on white sheets brain-birthed
Burned into existence
Descended to your heart open
And life-full as Mahler's Third
Became transfigured at your fingertips
As Schoenberg's Night
The baton arced, comet-ted in the supercharged air
Particles of light, quarks, muons of energy
Showered our beings
The universe engulfed transported into ethereal realms
Our souls star-steered
Now those stars are forever darkened
Notes rest mutely entombed beneath the earth
We gaze upon your leonine countenance
Nevermore your Talmudic tropes
Will our ears hear
You were a giant sequoia in the Muses' forest
May your soul find eternal peace
Beneath its autumnal leaves

— October 19, 1990

# In Memoriam
## *Primo Levi*
For Mo Z"L

Do you remember the night -
(perhaps there were stars twinkling)
you and I — listened to a reading
of a new translation of poems penned
by the Turin chemist
We sat in a semi-circle in the small
space that served as a bookstore
housing tomes now turned to pulp perhaps
as those were converted to ash
in another time another place
We listened into the night until the end —
when I had to ask — and so looking into
her eyes I entreated: *Do you think it was
an accident or did he really commit ...*
She paused, looking into my eyes —
eternity suspended in the night sky just beyond —
*I believe it was intentional* — or words to that effect —
words that I knew would be spoken —
but you see — I HAD to ask —
to have my suspicions confirmed
doubt sealed shut like a coffin
We left you and I —
perhaps gazing above
at the stars twinkling in the sky

In another time — another place —
we would have worn
stars "protecting" our breasts
mine a purple (not a pink) triangle
bisected by a yellow one each
supported by a cloth cane
sewn in for good measure
there would have been no
moments of reprieve for us
as in the end there were none for him whose
re-awakening only brought the sleep of death
you and I — we live in this time,
in this place and so we hear or read the words
produced by the alchemy of imagination
and neuro-transmitters/eye-hand
co-ordination and culture
commerce and curiosity
words given life on the mute page
vocalized vibrating vivified reverberating
in the small space on Newbury St.
the words written in the language of Dante
(twisted in the mouth of Mussolini into a
perverted hexagonal cross)
circle in the air that we breathe
transmuted into talismans of truth that we
wear on our hearts
hearts that beat
as those stars in the night sky

# PAS DE DEUX

I danced to the rhythm of my soul until I saw L.
who gracefully executed her heart's desire
in unsyncopated beats her body
flowed as an undulating current of
kinetic quiescence
her soul and her body as one
and my *anima* — imprisoned within my body
my body not as <u>animated</u> —
yes think movement — the divine creative spark
that gives life to black lines on the page
Disney as *deus*
my body animated but not to the degree I
would desire and so jealousy and rage
alchemically transmute my light and spirit
into leaden emotion for my body feels
its limbs are as lead
movement is syncopated between
inspiration and execution
the beat is skipped as my body tries to
catch my spirit disjunction not conjunction results
abnormal alchemy: jealousy and rage fill
the transparent vessels to bursting
until I say in the holy tongue
*lashon ha-kodesh Di!* Enough!
so that I want to die
as God should have commanded:
Enough! so that the holy light would
not shatter the vessels
but it did and God saw
that it was not good

Will my vessel shatter?
It is already broken and I cannot fix it
I can only redeem the scattered sparks
of light that I encounter here and there
My shadow self lurks in the corner of the studio
black as death blackened ebony
as the dark energy dark matter
comprising 95.1% of the universe
my shadow lurks over my spirit —
scythe in hand I wrestle it as best I can
victory in abeyance at least Jacob extracted a blessing
Can I extract the scintillating spot of gold
clenched within the skeletal hand?
I do not want to dance this *pas de deux*
let me banish my pernicious partner
to the oblivion of space
else that is where my soul shall reside
I must reach for the stars
else I crumble into the dust
And yet: from dust we come
to the stardust shall we return

— February 5, 1998

# SHIR HA-MA‘ALOT
## A SONG OF ASCENTS

I wander the universe in search of the
cosmic ladder
*sulam shel shalshelet ha-Kabbalah*
a ladder of chains of tradition
of mystic mystery every rung a heart
expansive as the universe
I climb that ladder
Jacob's ladder my ladder
*sulam shel Shalom*
the ladder of peace of *Shalom Shalom*'s
ladder Gemini twins atop its binary poles
*Hokhmah hesed netzah* open flowing
energy courses down its right side
*binah gevurah hod* focused reserved
current secrets itself descending alongside
for the pristine moment of revelation
Where am I?
situated ever so precipitously in-between
alighting on *tife'ret*
straddling *yesod* precisely *yesod*
magnificently mediating mid point
magically majestically messianically
mindful mirror *mayim* waters of life
male and female flowing ever so
quiescently from the Tree of Life
germinating Gemini — poles of the
universe left and right male and female
*yin* and *yang* contraction and expansion

I fly as Mercury from one extreme
to the other fluid fluctuating free
frolicking fitful finite focused
fizzled and fucked
(in every sense of the word
except the physical)
my heels restrained as Jacob's
damn that greedy Esau!
couldn't he have waited
like I should have waited —
three months more and now
I have paid too high a price —
if only I had known —
Fuck! Fuck! Fuck!
a curse for each month
lost in the womb of time
tethered chained to a body
that only desires the defeat of its defects
I navigate the cosmos like Richard III
my *neshamah* for a neo-natal neuron!
my *neshamah?* no but I would exchange
its equal to balance gracefully as Nijinsky
I desperately want to make the exchange
Gazing into the reflected mirror of my heart
my Double my gemini twin kisses me
on my lips guilessly gesturing:
You cannot
As Adam and Eve cast their eyes
downward I scrutinize the black vault
suspended above *terra infirma*
the land of the infirm

The vault contains the key the cipher
that opens all doors K. only had to knock
and the portal would have opened
as easily as a lover's lips part those
of their soul mate

Shalom ben Aharon ve-Beilah
— April 3, 1998

## BI-POLAR STREAM OF CONSCIOUSNESS

Gemini germination seed two seeds twins
my consciousness/unconscious wrestling?
embracing the dance one two three
one two three
two halves joined together
conjoined *conjunctio*
the marriage the consummation merger
then separation distinctness blackness
two lights two stars one greater one lesser
sun moon masculine feminine moon (light) light/shadow
polarities distance never reach the goal
(like K.) don't say that!
belief in self   groundless?
*terra firma* openness to sky heaven God *YH YH & VH*
liminality the doorstep
the threshold threshold of
consciousness of awareness
fluidity of the letters concepts
line demarcation boundary
Thou shalt/Thou shalt not
commandment *mitzvah*
Sinai God is with me God is with us
We are God God is us
Silence space time mystery infinity
The clock ticks The bell tolls
Ding-dong Ping-pong
The ball is in your court Court of Justice

Court of God Game Set Match
The earth is a globe Globe Theatre
Shakespeare Bard Hamlet
To be or not to be
Tomorrow and tomorrow
and tomorrow creeps in this petty
place from day to day
day to night light and shadow shadow self
struggle vanquish shadow accept shadow
the embrace back to the Beginning
the primordial point
point of existence

# UNION

God's light illuminates the Tree of Life
the Tree of Knowledge of Good and Evil
rooted deep in the earth its fruit redolent
of wisdom succulently sweet
Desire stirs and is awakened
limbs ache to embrace the other
pluck the fruit from the Tree
merge unite embrace the Truth
(what is the Truth?)
beating in the heart of the cosmos
canopied with stars light of God
carbon fire blaze Torah
Torah from the Big Bang
Torah secreted inside elementary particles
muons pisons bosons quanta of energy
building blocks of the universe
text letters tradition
latticed letters scaffolding a structured universe
tales chain of tradition links
Jacob's ladder structured from the TEXT
the omphalmos of the universe
Torah unravels from the apple peel
twisting like a DNA helix helixing
like a Möbius strip
text in our genes splicing interstices
G B A D protein enzymes
'aleph bet gimmel dalet
(a door) four letters four worlds

# 'EIKHAH 3:65

For Reb Diane

I write — indict these words in the haze of liminal
consciousness sleep crouches at the lintel of my awareness
as sin that crouches at the door God's admonishment to
Cain the first murderer a shedder of blood reddening the
earth with the effluvium of his jealousy
Jealousy begotten and begotten through the generations
until it too crouches at the door of Bar-Kamtza
As Cain betrayed Abel Bar-Kamtza betrayed us
the fires of *sin'at chinam*
spread from house to house extinguishing
love ravaging compassion immolating hope
*Ve-'ani b'tokh ha-golah* and I — I am in the midst of exile
Exiled from my body
Exiled from my soul
Exiled from my spirit
And my heart? Maintain a steadfast heart in me oh *YAH*
Give THEM anguish of heart ('Eikhah 3:65)
For I like Abel *Hevel* have been betrayed
All is futility *Havel havalim* in any event

Ahavah tikvah rachamim
Love hope compassion imprisoned in the
walls of flame engulfing Yerushalayim
ascend on the wings of the keys consigned
heavenwards by the Cohen Gadol
And I — imprisoned in my body
A body that cannot run or dance or respond
to the longings of its soul
perched now on the crenellated
ramparts of Yerushalayim
Shekhinah bereft of
Ha-Kadosh Baruch Hu
Her tears fill my heart until it
threatens to burst
Dima'ot Shekhinah tears higher than those of malakhim
Who can stand only in impotent dumbfoundment
at Yerushalayim's desolation

— July 4, 2003

# THE BLESSING

At the Yabbock River
I am Alone.

Whirling
Van-Gogh stars
puncture the incorrigible black
night.

Suddenly
You apear
plunging into the
life-current
arresting its flow
confronting me in the dark
of night as Ya'akov
met the angelic Messenger
of God.

But You are not
Ya'akov's angel.
You are the *Satan*,
the Adversary,
besting me once (or twice)
slugging it out night after night
encounter after encounter
like Sissyphus
condemned by the gods.

And I —
condemned also?

Both of us
locked in struggle.
As crooked Ya'akoov struggled,
he was made straight.
But I am made
crooked, off-course,
not yet limping
(Ya'akov's parting gift)
That comes later.

Black sky lightens
Flouresces to royal blue
Burnt orange streaks
the horizon.

You, Saturn-Chronos
Devourer of children
importune me:
"Let me go:
the dawn is breaking."

"I will not let You go
until You release me."

And You -
"Impossible — my nature compels
me to drive you as
a master his slave."

"Then bless me or
I battle You forever."

"No more shall your name
be called Struggler.
You shall be in harmony, not discord
with the world.
Completeness— Wholeness —
will envelop you
as a *tallit* envelops
a communer with God.
Shalom shall be
your name."

Thus, clothed in
my new name
as Joseph wrapped
in his coat of
many colors,
I freed the
Adversary
Who left me
limping
as Ya'akov
who struggled with God
thus becoming
the father of our people
Yisra'el.

— Shalom ben Aharon ve-Beilah

## TWO HANDS
### FOR DAD Z"L

Your hands intertwined with the two
white hands of the alarm clock
positioning the long arrow at 12
the short arrow at 1 then 2
patiently transmitting the mystery/mastery
of time until my eyes shine with wonder
wonder at the mental acrobatics marshaled
counting not just past 10, but 20, 30, 40,
speeding past 50, 60, 70, right
thru 80, 90 to 100 and then again and again
the red hand of the speedometer
on the tan dash of your 1963 turquoise Buick LeSabre,
on the black dash of your 1966 Buick Wildcat flying past 70,
then 80  approaching 85 my small plaid cap borne away on
rushing wind the excitement on your face that had seen
Senator Jack Kennedy campaigning Judy Garland singing
"all night" at Boston Garden she who had traversed that
endless corridor in the Holy of Holies of the Emerald City the
Emerald City (home to Boston's Irish) that beckoned you to
work each day at 284
Washington St./10 Milk St. 8th floor
(HA6-0868) I'd walk down that endless
corridor from the elevator your frosted glass door
at its end proclaiming
GRAY AND GRAY (why name a business after colors Black
and Black or White and White would do equally as well
as would Green and Green) the black and beige tax code
volumes sequestered behind glass doors the *sanctum
sanctorum* of the conference room my spirits as high as the

helium balloons anchored to the double
portmanteau doors after a visit to the circus
doors that opened to fairy tale lands the land of Oz you
and mom and Danny Kaye serving as sentries to my starry
imagination believing that the Wizard/Professor Marvel in
his air ballon could be a *deus ex machina* for Dorothy and
Toto as you were that summer at camp rescuing me from a
two week exile from home we dined on sable and whitefish
sandwiches arrayed on your Indian blanket on the grass
grass and soil that yielded to a shovel at the site of the not
yet new home of Temple Beth David breaking new ground
as I still try to do  the two of us adorned in golden tuxedoes
that night of the day I became a man golden as the sunlight
on that day in April when we beheld the panoramic City on
a Hill from the 50th floor of the Prudential Tower golden as
Caribbean light of Curacao
the bright yellow walls of Mikveh Yisrael synagogue
sanded floors *Shema' Yisra'el*
a Hebrew *E Pluribus Unum* morning light on Jerusalem
stone the stone of the Western Wall your hands kiss its face
your face framed in the 3 inch square window of the AT&T
videophone at the New York World's Fair you in '39 you
and I in '65 the Futurama pavilion the kitchen of the future
featuring microwave ovens and a smiling model a model
world it's a small one after all
Walt would know for he brought us Mary Poppins larger than
life  she who would ascend to Heaven where Prometheus
dwelt now residing at Rockefeller Center my eyes dazzled
by the Rockettes Radio City Music Hall kicking as high as the
icicles tethered to the roof of a white ranch house ephemeral
frozen treasure spirited to me by you at my behest cradled in
terry towels as you were in your Indian blanket
sparkling before my eyes  eyes that marveled at fires
warming us in a brick hearth  eyes that marveled at a toy

rocket built by you and me for a first grade science fair  eyes
that marveled at puzzles assembled piece by piece - can we
ever put all the pieces together? — Here — I have related
some of them  linked one by one
piece interlocking piece memory interlocking memory time
interlocking time its paternal hands shelter your heart
in mine

All my love,
Ken

# NOTES

### Garments: *Va-Yeshev*

This poem is based on Genesis 37. Joseph is considered a *tzaddik* in Jewish tradition because he resisted the advances of Potiphar's wife. The *sefirah* of *yesod* in the Tree of Life is the archetype of Joseph. This *sefirah* denotes sexuality.

### A Tower of Bricks: A Tower of Strength: *Noah*

This poem is about Nimrod, ruler of Babylon and grandson of Noah. *Midrashim* about him relate that he built the Tower of Babel using slave labor, that as a fire worshipper he consigned Abraham (Abram) to the fire who survived thanks to the angel Gavriel and that Abram witnessed the Tower's construction. Babel is translated as: the gate of God.

### The Staff of Aaron: *Va-'Era'*

This poem is based on Exodus 7: 9-12 where God instructs Moses to tell Aaron to throw down his staff before Pharaoh. Aaron does so and the staff becomes a serpent swllowing the rods of Pharaoh's magicians. I allude to a *midrash* that speaks of Moses' staff being one of the ten things created before the first *Shabbat*. I also mention the burial place of Aaron on Mt. Hor. Aaron is the archetype of *Hod* (glory) in the Tree of Life.

### Light and Darkness: *Bo'*

Please note the substitution of "the Egyprians" in the quote of Exodus 13:2.

### The Palace: *Mishpatim*

I refer to the first translation of the Hebrew Bible into Greek (by 70 translators) and also allude to the numerical value of the Hebrew word for witness — 74 — because there are 74 individuals mentioned in this Torah portion.

### Holy Fire: *Va-Yakhel*

The first line of this poem is based on Exodus 35:3. I very much appreciate the collaboration of Reb Hanna Tiferet Siegel in helping me craft a suitable conclusion to this poem.

### Mother and Daughter: *Ba-Midbar*

This poem is based on Numbers 1-4:20. The tribes of Israel are camped around the *mishkan*. The poem also refers to the story of Dinah, sister of Shim'on and Levi in Genesis 34.

### Rav Kook Poem Cycle

These poems were composed in a redwood grove at a Baha'i retreat center in CA. Reb Itzchak Marmorstein taught a class on Rav Kook there. He asked us to write in this grove and these are the poems that bore seed there.

### Fruit

Paul Gaugin's 1892 painting "*Vahine no te Vi*" (Woman with Mango) inspired this poem.

### Union
### Pas De Deux
### Shir Ha-Ma'alot: *A Song of Ascents*
### Bi-polar Stream of Consciousness

These poems were all composed in a class taught by Julie Leavitt on Jungian Dance and Drama Therapy.

'Eikhah 3:65

This poem was composed as part of a class where each student picked a verse at random from The *Book of Lamentations ('Eikhah)* whose theme was "Bringing Our Bodies to Wholeness" taught by Reb Diane Elliot at the 2003 ALEPH Kallah.

Two Hands: *For Dad z"l*

This poem was written about six months before my father died. I read it to him at Pesach. His response was "lots of memories."

# GLOSSARY

*'afikoman* - the piece of *matzah* — unleavened bread that is hidden during the Pesach *Seder* for children to find and redeem.

*'aggadah* - Jewish legend and lore.

*'aleph beit gimmel dalet* - the first four letters of the Hebrew alphabet.

*'alef-bais* (Yiddish) - the first two letters of the Hebrew alpahabet, also the term for alphabet.

Apple Orchard - a term denoting Jewish mysticism.

*besamim* - spices.

*binah* - understanding — one of the ten mystical divine emanations of God.

*brit* - covenant, thus the circumcision ceremony ushering a male into the covenant.

*brit hadashah* - new covenant.

*hokhmah* - wisdom — one of the ten mystical divine emanations of God.

*Cohen Gadol* - High Priest.

Eliyahu Ha-Navi - Elijah the Prophet.

*Eretz zavat halav u-devash* - a land flowing with milk and honey.

*gevurah* - strength, judgement — one of the ten mystical divine emanations of God.

*Ha-Kadosh Baruch Hu* - The Holy One, Blessed be He (God) in Jewish mysticism, the masculine aspect of God.

*halachah, halakhah* - Jewish law literally, the path, the way.

*havdalah* - literally separation, the ceremony at the conclusion of the Sabbath denoting its end and the beginning of the week.

*heikhalot* - plural of *heikhal* — palace.

*Hesed* - compassion/grace/love — one of the ten mystical divine emanations of God.

*hitlahavut* - divine enthusiasm.

*hod* - glory — one of the ten mystical divine emanations of God.

*'Ir Shalem* - City of Peace - the root meaning of Yerushalayim, Jerusalem

*kav 'or 'ein sof* - the line of primordial light of God in God's most transcendent and unknowable aspect.

*kelipot* - shells, in Jewish mysticism the shells that contain the divine light of creation which we attempt to liberate by performing the commandments of God.

*keruvim* - divine beings, angels who guard the Tree of Life in the Garden of 'Eden and the Ark of the Covenant.

*ketubah* - marriage contract.

*kodesh kodashim* - The Holy of Holies, the most intimate, sacred part of the Holy Temple.

*Kol Nidre* - literally all vows, the evening service in which vows are annullled at the beginning of Yom Kippur, the Day of Atonement.

*korban* - offering, a sacrifice made in the Holy Temple, literally drawing near to God.

*lashon ha-kodesh* - Hebrew, the holy tongue.

*mal'akh* - mesenger, an angel (who brings a message from God).

*Malkhuyot* - the section of the Rosh Ha-Shanah service devoted to the sovereignty of God.

*Mashiah* - the Messiah.

*mayim* - water.

*mezzuzah* - the interior scroll housed in a casing placed on the doorpost of a home/building containing verses of Deuteronomy. It is believed that these verses confer protective power.

*minhah* - the afternoon service.

*mishkan* - the portable sanctuary which housed the Ark of the Covenant symbolizing God's presence as the Israelites made their Exodus trek.

*Mitzrayim* - literally, the Double Narrows signifying Egypt.

*mitzvah* - commandment of God, good deed.

Moshe Rabbenu - Moses our teacher.

*musaf* - the service after the morning service of *Shabbat* or another holiday.

*ne'ilah* - literally closing the concluding service of Yom Kippur in which the gates of repentance close. Tradition teaches that the gates of return to God are never closed.

*ner tamid* - the continually illuminated lamp of the synagogue known as the eternal lamp.

*neshamah* - soul, in Jewish mysticism, a level of soul.

*netzah* - endurance, victory, one of the ten mystical divine emanations of God.

*PaRDeS* - literally, orchard, Paradise — here, an acronym denoting the four aspects of Jewish text interpretation: *Peshat* - literal, *Remez* - hint thus, allegorical, *Drash (Midrash)* - connoting rabbinic exegesis/imaginative elaboration of the biblical text, *Sod* - mystical.

*rebbe* (Yiddish) - rabbi, respected person.

*reishit* - beginning.

Sambatyon River - a mythical river which spews fire and stones for 6 days and rests on the Sabbath.

*sefirot* - plural of *sefirah*, sphere thus the ten mystical divine emanations, qualities of God constituting the Tree of Life in Jewish mysticism.

*selihot* - a service during the penitential period of the year preceeding Rosh Ha-Shanah or after Rosh Ha-Shanah depending on rite observed.

*Shabbat* - the Sabbath.

*shaharit* - the morning service.

*Shekhinah* - the feminine aspect of God.

*shofarot* - plural of *shofar*, ram's horn thus the section of the Rosh Ha-Shanah service devoted to the shofar which is blown at the conclusion of the Rosh Ha-Shanah service before the *tashlikh* service of symbolically throwing away our imperfections, our missings of the mark.

*shalosh seudos* (Yiddish) - the third meal of *Shabbat*.

*sin'at chinam* - causeless hatred.

*sukkah* - a temporary structure erected during Sukkot (plural of *sukkah*) the Feast of Booths known in Christianity as Tabernacles reminiscent of the Israelites' construction of dwellings in the wilderness during the Exodus.

*tallit* - a prayer shawl which has four knotted fringes at each corner reminding Jews of God's commandments.

Talmud - the 63 tractates of Jewish law and legend created by the early rabbis after the destruction of the Second Temple.

*teki'ah* - a type of *shofar* blast.

*teshuvah* - turning to God and people in rectification of our human imperfections.

*tif'eret* - beauty, one of the ten mystical divine emanations of God.

*tzaddikim* - righteous people, in Hasidisdm those who intercede between a Hasid and God.

*tzel* - shadow.

*YAH* - a shortened form of the sacred four letter name of God *Y H V H*.

Yerushalayim - Jerusalem.

*yesod* - foundation, one of the ten mystical divine emanations of God.

*yetzer ha-ra'* - the evil inclination.

*yetzer ha-tzel* - my word for the Jungian concept of the shadow, our unconscious undesirable aspects of our self and our ego.

Yisra'el - Israel.

Yom Kippur - The Day of Atonement also At-one-ment, the holiest day of the Jewish year.

*zikhronot* - the section of the Rosh Ha-Shanah service focusing on memory.

Zohar - literally, splendor, radiance — thus the central work of Jewish mysticism.

*Ken Rosenstein*

# TIME, SPACE, AND SOUL

KEN ROSENSTEIN is a teacher of Integral thought and practice who holds an MA in Psychology and Spirituality from Lesley University. He writes creative Biblical exegesis *(midrash)* and teaches workshops that intertwine Judaism and psychology, and is currently a student in the Jewish Renwal ALEPH Rabbinic Program. Ken lives in Boston, Massachusetts.

www.ingramcontent.com/pod-product-compliance
Lightning Source LLC
LaVergne TN
LVHW011208080426
835508LV00007B/671